Table of Contents

Chivalry - The Knight before Christmas

"Some say that the age of chivalry is past, that the spirit of romance is dead. The age of chivalry is never past, so long as there is a wrong left unredressed on earth."

— Charles Kingsley

"I have been finding treasures in places I did not want to search. I have been hearing wisdom from tongues I did not want to listen. I have been finding beauty where I did not want to look. And I have

learned so much from journeys I

did not want to take. Forgive me,

O Gracious One; for I have been

closing my ears and eyes for too

long. I have learned that miracles

are only called miracles because

they are often witnessed by only

those who can see through all of

life's illusions. I am ready to see

what really exists on other side,

what exists behind the blinds, and

taste all the ugly fruit instead of

all that looks right, plump and

ripe."

— **Suzy Kassem, <u>Rise Up and Salute

the Sun: The Writings of Suzy

Kassem</u>**

Listening to

your heart

1334 and 2019 collide and mingle in The Knight before Christmas. The protagonists' worlds are so different that an airplane feels like a dragon to our knight Cole. The rules of gallantry have changed with rules to not put cheating "scoundrels" in the right place today, but I couldn't agree more with the knight that we wish things were better these days. Listening to your heart seems to be at the core of finding one's quest, which our true knight Cole cannot do at the start.

Things beyond our comprehension

"By that logic, only things you comprehend are possible" – which is what rings true even in the current world when you have discussions around what the future holds. Cole is left with no options to continue his quest if he has no idea about where he is going, like our lives, where many of us have no direction in terms of where we are going. But the point is we can't give up, just like Cole is advised to not give up in the movie.

Giving back

Christmas is a good time for giving back, and the philanthropic efforts by Brooke first to give a lost man home and her Christmas Eve feast shows all that Christmas is all about. And Christmas is also a time that reminds us of what makes us human beyond the regular markers of money, success, and relationships. It reminds us to

be good human beings.

Supporting

each other

The story is about believing in each other and supporting each other to become a better version of ourselves. Like all things in life, a significant life event like finding one's quest might be worthy, but it paled when compared to matters of the heart. That's what

Cole realizes from his brother Geoffrey.

Progressive values

Though the movie blends a by-gone era with the present world, the values are relatively progressive. For example, the knight moves for his one true love and decides to find a vocation to suit her current disposition. Though we usually don't expect such liberal values from someone

from 1334, it is still commendable

what the movie can achieve by

articulating this rather

progressive notion.

Renaissance man/ woman

We are given the image of a renaissance man who is both a baker and a fighter. This does away with the notion that a true knight in every sense of the word has to be a mere macho person devoid of the humanistic qualities that make him whole. Also, the notion of love as a quest for a man is relatively progressive. We usually see depictions of men striving for success alone in the contemporary world.

Self-healing - Dear Zindagi (Dear Life)

"What happens when people open their hearts?"

"They get better."

— **Haruki Murakami, <u>Norwegian Wood</u>**

"Pain is a pesky part of being human, I've learned it feels like a stab wound to the heart, something I wish we could all do without, in our lives here. Pain is a sudden hurt that can't be escaped. But then I have also learned that because of pain, I can feel the beauty, tenderness, and freedom of healing. Pain feels like a fast stab wound to the heart. But then healing feels like the wind against your face when you are spreading your wings and flying through the air! We may not have wings growing out of our backs, but healing is the closest thing that will give us that wind against our faces."

— C. JoyBell C.

Forward-thinking

The movie starts off with a forward-thinking woman being the cinematographer. We get a retake of a film that we go through in our daily lives. After a man cheats on a woman and they reconcile, the woman seeks an open relationship seeing that it is getting her nowhere. Again, when the movie producer points out that people would love to work with her because she is attractive, she is offended.

Juggling personal and professional

Kaira has a fling with a guy on a business trip while she is already in a relationship. We don't know what's going on in her mind when she takes this step. Her best friends are against her decision to break up with a nice guy, but she goes against their judgment. The fact that she is juggling both a professional and personal relationship with her producer sends us the alarm bells. Still, Kaira seems to be oblivious to this. It looks like she wants to be with Raghuvender, but he seems to have other plans.

Going through

it

In the daily humdrum of life, it is hard to empathize with someone if you haven't gone through what they go through. Kaira goes through the same phase in life as Sid when Raghu cheats on her just as she had cheated on Sid. Conventional wisdom is hard to sink in unless we go through the

actual struggles in life like Kaira

does.

The easy path may not be unsuitable

Sometimes in life, we think that the road ahead is filled with difficulties, especially if we have to adapt to other people's notion of what it takes to be successful. Still, Dr. Khan teaches us that the most straightforward path could as quickly lead us to our goal as the difficult path. Therefore, if we are not ready to take the problematic route, it doesn't hurt to choose a way that feels more comfortable to us.

Gender and scrutiny

As the movie is set in India and women might fall under more scrutiny to play traditional gender roles, a one-night stand might come with a lot less social sanction. Dr. Khan does not fall prey to this paradigm. His ultimate takeaway is creating an analogy with testing chairs till we find one

that suits our apartment and adds

comfort. Relationships are similar

- we have to kiss many frogs till

we find our prince.

Parental neglect

Parental neglect goes a long way in people's lives. We find it difficult to forgive our parents because they abandoned us at a critical juncture in our lives when we were least capable of fending for ourselves. Superficial issues like failing a small test can seem more substantial to folks than years of neglect that brought out this happening. In short, sometimes, the same thing might not mean the same to everyone. Though a child may not see through these happenings objectively, it is possible to discern these failings of another human (our parents) as an adult and consider these flaws normal. Life comes easy when we can resolve our issues with ourselves - no explanations to others are

necessary.

Opening up

- To All the

Boys I've

Loved Before

"Love is supposed to be based on trust, and trust on love, it's something rare and beautiful when people can confide in each other without fearing what the other person will think."

— **E.A. Bucchianeri, <u>Brushstrokes of a Gadfly</u>**

"What's the point of opening yourself up to your friends if they don't notice your vulnerable state? The point of it all is to love

friends completely and utterly, at

their best and worst, and to love

more than just the good things."

— **Arka Pain**

A crush so strong

It is easy to relate to Lara Jean when she talks about a crush so strong that we feel the urge to vent it out in some creative form, and that's precisely what this movie starts off with. But, of course, there is no way that it will lead to something more than that.

Still, the plot brings in her ever-popular little sister Kitty who knows just how to get Lara Jean actually talking with the real world. As her secret is out, we find the forces of nature play out.

Authentic connections

The movie beautifully shows how people genuinely connect and bond over moments of truth, mutually shared experiences, and candor. The lead lady opens and shows a part of herself that we had not seen earlier. She is not afraid of standing up to the most popular girl in school. She is doing

all this to help her keep her lifelong

friendship with her best friend

Josh intact.

Love and loss

Interwoven in the story are themes of loss and what it does to us in handling our fears. There is also this fear of losing someone in a relationship after we have been in too deep. This is doubly painful for someone who has recently had a loss. Lara Jean is afraid of losing someone special in her life. This fear keeps her from actual

relationships though she loves
dreaming and fantasizing about
them.

Opening up

Also, sub-themes include the transient nature of some feelings while growing up and in our teenage years. It is relatable when Lara Jean speaks of her initial feelings about Josh and how they faded away with time to leave traces of deep friendship alone. Also interwoven are themes of jealousy and rivalry and how narratives may be twisted to suit one's own agenda. At the end of the movie, we appreciate how opening up about our feelings at different points in our lives can open us to connection and growth. Though we may not always have a sister like Kitty, who is competent to figure it out, our inspiration will come from different sources in our lives.

Forging one's own path - Enola Holmes

"You must forge your own path for it to mean anything."

— **Rick Riordan, <u>The Lost Hero</u>**

"No one saves us but ourselves. No one can and no one may. We ourselves must walk the path."

— **Gautama Buddha, <u>Sayings Of Buddha</u>**

Doing well on your own

The movie starts with the revelation that the name Enola is alone spelled backward, and with her mother's reinforcement that she could do very well on her own, we are not surprised that the heroine holds her own. However, after her mother disappears, she is forced to do the exact opposite of her feminist upbringing and get ready for society, that is, to attract men. The movie gives us a historical glimpse of the women's rights movement in the late 1800s to early 1900s.

Finding the strength

The beauty of the movie lies in Enola's realization that she has the strength to stop the attackers from harming the Viscount. But, unfortunately, the young Viscount does not himself have the power to prevent them. There is an exchange of traditional gender roles here, and it is heartening to see that in action. During the women's movement, the situation can be summarized as: "you have no interest in changing a world that suits you so well" but Enola is on her way to change that.

Larger

implications

The boarding school that Enola is forced into aims to train girls into "acceptable wives and responsible mothers," far detached from the world that her mother had envisioned for her. The Viscount and his father's decision to pass the liberal bill is tied up with the disappearance of the Viscount and the attempt to kill him. In short, the family feud has more significant political implications for the people of England. This also mainly concerns women, as they would have had a say in the governance of England if they got the right to vote. It is a sweet attempt to convey the succinct message that the personal is political.

The personal is indeed political

The whole idea that his 16-year-old younger sister beats Sherlock Holmes at solving the case shows us a great role model in a male-dominated occupation. The movie's central theme revolves around a mother's struggle to build a better world for her daughter - one in which she could bring her total self to society. Sometimes being political might not mean engaging in a civil disobedience movement. This is what the movie Enola Holmes can achieve. Being political might also mean helping the political party pass a liberal agenda. The idea of forging one's own path does not mean being lonely but rather is a route to finding the freedom to be

of use to the larger society.

Self-discovery - The Perfect Date

"We shall not cease from exploration

And the end of all our exploring

Will be to arrive where we started

And know the place for the first time."

— **T. S. Eliot, <u>Four Quartets</u>**

"It takes courage...to endure the sharp pains of self discovery rather than choose to take the dull pain of unconsciousness that would last the rest of our lives."

— **Marianne Williamson, <u>A Return to Love: Reflections on the Principles of "A Course in Miracles"</u>**

Traditional markers of success

The movie starts off with Brook going after all the traditional markers of success in high school: getting into an Ivy League school, having the most popular girl as your girlfriend, and driving the fastest car. He thinks that getting into Yale will prove that he is someone special. However, we see that Celia is on the opposite side of the spectrum where Ivy League degrees or her fancy upbringing doesn't seem to excite her.

Self – discovery as a lifelong process

At last, wisdom dawns on him when he realizes from his father that self-discovery is a lifelong process and the admission essay to

Yale has to be a work in progress. He realizes that being accepted for what he is not won't be a great choice. He will have to keep up this pretense for life which seems suffocating. But, on the other hand, he can understand his true feelings for Celia, with whom he has always been himself and who accepts him for who he is.

Being yourself

Secondary themes evolve around being a different person for different people in our lives. One might feel it is possible to be someone to suit every person in our life. Still, the pretense becomes too burdensome and finally gives way and is discovered as a lie. Pretending to be someone you are not to get admission might be a temporary fix. Still, it does not solve the long-term problem that you might not actually fit in an environment that does not accept people like you.

What makes us whole

Lasting hollowness can be a symptom of lacking authentic human connections and cannot be merely filled by amassing traditional markers of success. This is what Brook realizes when he is estranged from Celia and gets to reflect on his self-centered actions earlier. He also understands the true essence of friendship with Murph with whom he became distanced after getting more and more involved in the chaperone app Stand-in. The coming-of-age movie is a good saga of self-discovery and realization that dawns on us during our teenage years and continues throughout life.

Spontaneity

- Princess

Switch

"Be spontaneous!

Never be afraid to try new things

or find new ways!

Don't let routine ruin your life!"

— **Mouloud Benzadi**

"Artists strive to free this

true and spontaneous self in their

work. Creativity, meditation are

ways of freeing an inner voice."

— **Gloria Steinem, <u>Revolution from</u>**

<u>Within: A Book of Self-Esteem</u>

Life is what happens when you are busy making plans

When a baker in Chicago finds out that she has won a chance to participate in an internationally famous cooking contest, she is hardly excited. It would mean closing the shop for Christmas. "Life is what happens when you are busy making plans" is what a considerate man tells her twice while she is out shopping. The Duchess of Montenaro - Margaret is the exact opposite and wants to spontaneously lead the life of an average person when her fiancé Edward is away on a business trip.

Whose

business?

The movie tends to achieve the progression of the feminist idea that the duchess takes some ownership of the matters of the state and gets involved in activities that matter to the state, like charity. Like Edward's grandmother, who was ahead of her times, Stacy would rule with progressive ideas in place for the state. As such, she is not the type to let the prince take complete control of the state without any didactic advice from her while she attends to personal matters alone like planning her wedding.

An ordinary life

On the other hand, Margaret blended well with the everyday world. She was entering a marriage only because she did not want to let down her deceased parents. They told her that marriage is a medium by which nations come together, and she should do it as a matter of duty. This act of duty would not have helped anyone as it is devoid of love. She realizes that she is in love with Kevin after spending some time with him and his daughter Olivia.

Spontaneity

None of this would have happened without a dose of spontaneity from Margaret. She dared to do things differently to gain a new perspective of life and live the life of someone she would never be and, in the process, discovered the life of someone she would love to be. Stacy learned that not everything in life can be planned, and life does happen when

you are busy making plans.

Anybody can be a princess

Secondary themes that emerge during the movie are the meaning of the term princess. When Stacy tells the girl in the orphanage that anyone who cares for others is a princess at heart and that we all choose what we want to be in life, we are introduced to the term's true

meaning.

Spontaneity and the corporate world

Being spontaneous is usually not a positive thing as an adult, especially in the corporate world, which is obsessed with to-do lists, personal digital assistants, and organizers. However, sometimes it does help to let fate take its own course by letting go.

The right to be

a free bird

Another theme that emerges is the resignation to our fate. Sometimes we feel that once we reach a particular social standing, we must stick to it no matter what, even if the decision does not make us happy. However, this movie teaches us that this necessarily does not have to be the

case and frees us from this

quandary.

Taming our gifts: Fate - The Winx Saga

"My takeaway from all of Ophelia's sessions was that life favored value. The world was bursting with opportunity. If you didn't like who you were, it was time to reinvent yourself and try again. It was a disservice to the universe to cheat everyone of your talents. And if you were at your wit's end, thinking you had nothing to offer, it was essential to cultivate value within yourself in order to move forward. In order

to live beyond existence. In order
to turn your pain into something
beautiful."

— **Fran Seen, <u>Lionheart</u>**

"The world awaits your
products. Humanity lives in eager
expectation of your products.
Begin to convert your time into
products. Begin to gain the
mastery over your talents and
gifting."

— **Sunday Adelaja**, <u>**How To Become**</u>

<u>**Great Through Time Conversion:**</u>

<u>**Are you wasting time, spending**</u>

<u>**time or investing time?**</u>

Controlling magic

Bloom is new to the otherworld as she was only introduced to Alfea a couple of months ago by the school's headmistress. The headmistress highlights that the magic needs to be used slowly and safely, standing as a metaphor for realizing our gifts at a steady pace that doesn't overwhelm us in the process. The headmistress reminds Bloom that she came to Alfea because she knew that she had no other choice or that it would be very hard for her if she didn't know how to control her magic.

The business of being social

Bloom's parents insist that she be social, something she found hard to achieve in California. Bloom needs a safe place to practice her magic - where she can be herself and get the answer she needs - away from her classmates. Emotions control fairy magic, which is all she needs to get started. She started a fire and tried to hold it with both her hands but lost control till her friend decided to come and help her. If not tempered in a didactic environment, our gifts can be hard to hone if we don't have expert guidance.

The outburst of magic

Sometimes, we are forced to be someone we are not in our teenage years. This can cause emotional distress. When the person concerned is gifted or magical, it can also lead to a dangerous outburst - untamed and uncontrolled, which led to a terrible fire in the case of Bloom.

Bloom hears from Aisha that she is a changeling - a fairy baby exchanged with a human baby at birth because of how powerful her magic is without even trying. This is true for women in the current generation. We find so many gifts to lead the world in different areas today - arts, business and technology, et al. - which were repressed in our grandmother's days.

Figuring out our path

The burned ones or the fictitious villains that emerge in the show can be ruthless but pose the right amount of challenge to Bloom to uncover her gifts and find her strengths. Through a complex web of interrelationships playing out - we know that the future is not safe for Alfea. Still, we have

confidence in our girls and their

classmates to figure out the path

for themselves.

Discovering

our roots

The story unfolds when the rumor that Bloom is a changeling spreads throughout the school, making Bloom even more anxious to discover her roots. This makes her cross paths with Beatrix, who tells her the story of Aster Dell, where she was born. Both Beatrix and Bloom's families lost their lives in Aster Dell when the burned ones decided to take refuge in this location, and the arm guards of Alfea agreed to hush up the war crime. In this ordeal, the fairy families lost their lives in Alfea, and only these two could survive due to Rosalind changing her heart at the last minute. These memories were etched into Beatrix which she recounted to Bloom. This shows that the authority figures in the school were lying to

Bloom all this time.

Crossroads at who to trust

Often in our lives, we find it at crossroads as who to trust, but we have to trust the process, which holds true for Bloom because the more sources she exposes herself to, the closer to the truth she gets. Also, various themes emerge in the story. Tera's heartbreak with one of the specialists shows us a lot about teenage peer pressure and how it affects the lives of teenagers. Alongside this, we see the love story of Musa and Tera's brother unfold. Finally, we see how conscious Musa is to own up to Tera, giving us a wholesome glimpse into the tangle of teenage relationships, both romantic and sisterhood.

The struggle for power

A glimpse into Queen Luna and Dowling's tug of war gives us a view of the future where Alfea may not be heading into sunny times. This is at a critical juncture where five burned ones have already been sighted. The power balance and the need to restore it will bring more characters into the picture like Rosalind. This is a metaphor for the struggle for power in the real world and the complications that come with it.

Sisterhood overrides all

Frequently, we can't help but talk about politics at work which colors everything we do in life and leaves us feeling frustrated. We feel as if we are losing control and heading towards a closed door. One can, however, not help but feel hopeful with the sisterhood of interwoven relationships and the fact that they are a force to reckon with to bring in better prospects of what's coming next.

Discovering

our powers

Bloom discovers ancient fairy magic after spending some time with Rosalind, one of the most famous fairies of her time and her ex-headmistress. After she transforms into an actual fairy, she can fight the burned ones and save the school from disaster - a metaphor for the power within us to change into our best selves. Bloom can also take the danger away from the school and fight it herself after she discovers that they are after her. This is again a metaphor for her sense of responsibility. She is not selfishly obsessed with her roots and putting the school and the rest of their lives in grave danger in the process.

Testing the limits of our knowledge

The show plays around the limits of our knowledge, where everyone is taking actions based on whatever information they have before them without any white or black themes. It is hard to figure out who is on the good side and who is on the bad when the good and bad pieces repeatedly change when new information presents itself. This is akin to the real world when our opinion about public personas repeatedly changes when further information is given to us in the media. When our decisions are so fragile and so dependent on the current context, it is hard to plan our way ahead into the future. As new information presents itself, our decisions will change as they did for our powerful fairy Bloom.

Finding

your voice –

Queen

"A girl should be two things: who and what she wants."
— **Coco Chanel, <u>The Gospel According to Coco Chanel: Life Lessons from the World's Most Elegant Woman</u>**

"It is easier to live through someone else than to complete yourself. The freedom to lead and plan your own life is frightening if you have never faced it before. It

is frightening when a woman
finally realizes that there is no
answer to the question 'who am I'
except the voice inside herself."

— **Betty Friedan**

Too good for you

The movie starts with the hustle-bustle of a typical Indian wedding preparation where our 'Queen' Rani is shown full of excitement for the future. Her fiancé, however, informs her in a somewhat detached fashion that the marriage needs to be called off.

Given his recent stint in London, he is now too good for her. However, we are too shocked when we find our Queen pleading with him to marry her to avoid embarrassing everyone. Our protagonist has led a sheltered life which has led to her devaluing herself and losing self-respect.

Choosing

freedom

Fast forward - she decides to still go on her honeymoon trip, which was already booked. Whether she treats it as a way to reconcile with her fiancé or to find her own path - we are not too sure. We are, however, hopeful that she grows up to be a better judge of character than she has been before. Here, she comes across Vijaylaxmi, who is the very epitome of what she is not - an effervescent and confident single mom. Rani here is introduced to a world where she has to stop being judgmental and repressed. While drunk, she confides that she has always been an obedient girl. Unfortunately, this didn't work out well for her. She even asked her fiancé Vijay whether she could have a career which he promptly

refused, and she obliged.

Building your identity

While hanging out with her roommates in Amsterdam, she realizes that she needs to build her own identity. So she participates in a cooking competition which gains traction. She also ends up crossing paths with her fiancé, who wants to reconcile with her seeing that she has changed and become good enough for him again. She, however, delays decision-making and attends a farewell rock show with her roommates, who she might never see again. This shows a mature woman who values friendship and respects herself, so our admiration for her grows.

Being strong

After returning to India, she returns her engagement ring to Vijay and thanks him for calling off the marriage as none of her transformations would have happened had she not faced adversity. We see her blossoming into a strong woman with a mind of her own, who is not desperate to gain others' approval. After learning from strong women like

Vijaylaxmi, who supports her child,

or Roxette, who educates her two

younger sisters, she imbibes the

lessons to be strong herself.

Thank You

I am thankful to my cover artist G3 Studios (Covertopia.com), for providing a magical glimpse into the book. I couldn't be more grateful to goodreads.com to be an excellent repository for quotes to phrase what I am trying to get at and to Netflix for providing engaging content to engage with.

Further, I am thankful to my friends and family for their incredible support as I sat down to draft the manuscript. I am grateful to my beautiful readers for taking the time to give me constructive feedback to help me grow. Finally, I am thankful to God for surrounding us with hope, challenges, optimism, and instilling in us a can-do attitude.